I0412820

ISBN-13: 978-1499262100

ISBN-10: 1499262108

**Disclaimer:** The author has put all his efforts to present valid, accurate and fresh information to the user. But due to the changing nature of the book subject (herbs), the author cannot be held responsible for the success or failure the reader will achieve after applying the methods to grow any herb. You own your results and you must handle them.

**Printed by CreateSpace, An Amazon.com company**

# Table of Contents

# Growing Aphrodisiac Damiana at Home!

Herbs, oils and other aphrodisiacs!
Highly recommended, please visit this
link:

http://hyperdeals.biz/go/17/

# Intro

**So you want to increase sexual potency? Then** try drinking some Damiana tea!

Even better, try to grow this shrub at home. It is a strong herb that will grow easily if you spend a few minutes to take care of it (water it). It requires very little maintenance comparing to other plants.

Damiana has always been famous for its **aphrodisiac** effects to the body and sexual mood of the human who consumes the herb. It has been known since the time of the ancient S. American civilizations (Maya, Aztecs). Back then it was also used as the most powerful aphrodisiac.

**Today it still used for the same reasons. As an aphrodisiac!** Apart from its marvelous effects in boosting sexual performance, Damiana can become the Queen of every garden with its beautiful yellow flowers and its nice scent. You simply cannot avoid this plant!

Let's also read the definition that Wikipedia gives for Damiana:

*"Turnera diffusa, known as Damiana, is a shrub native to southwestern Texas in the United States, Central America, Mexico, South America, and the Caribbean. It belongs to the family Passifloraceae."*

In this book I will give as much information as I can about growing Damiana from the comfort of your own home (in a pot or pots). I will try to present everything in a step by step manner.

Keep in mind that (for some reason I will explain later) Damiana is considered illegal to grow in some countries/states, for example Louisiana USA. But in most places, this powerful herb is 100% legal and ready to produce its wonderful effects to those who consume it.

**So, what are we waiting for? Let's begin revealing how to grow this magical plant/flower!**

# Step 1: Types of Damiana plants.

As you can imagine, in order to grow Damiana you have to find the right type of plant (seedling) or seeds (start from scratch).

**There are two types of Damiana plants:**

- *Turnera Aphrodisiaca Damiana* (used as a powerful aphrodisiac as its name implies)

- *Turnera Diffusa Damiana* (used for herbal healing and as a natural anti-depressant. Also counts as an aphrodisiac)

In our case we want to find some *Turnera Aphrodisiaca Damiana* plants or seeds (you can grow both types if you like, they will work miracles as an aphrodisiac). Some people use any of the two types as an aphrodisiac.

Now, when you want to grow it you can either buy a pre-grown plant or plants. But you can always start it from point zero (recommended) by acquiring and planting seeds yourself.

So, first decide which method you will use. I recommend starting from seeds but this choice is yours!

Let's review both methods...

# Step 2a: Growing Damiana from a pre-grown plant (seedling)

**You will need:**

- A Damiana Seedling (pre-grown plant)

- A pot of suitable size

- Some soil suitable for plant growing. You can use a mixture of soil and gravel.

After you have everything in place, cover half (or so) the pot with the soil. Then take the Damiana seedling from the old pot and place it in the center of the new pot. Finally cover the root system with the rest of the soil.

You want to make sure the entire root system is covered with soil.

Also, place the Damiana plant gently into the new pot and don't press the soil when covering the roots.

Then water the pot immediately but with great care. After that, water daily or before the soil starts to become dry.

Remember, this plant loves sun light and it can get as much as you can possibly give it! This also means that you should not leave it outside the house during cold seasons.

# Step 2b: Growing Damiana from seeds

**You will need:**

- The Damiana seeds of your choice.

- A few suitable pots for planting the seeds.

- Some suitable soil for plant growing.

To find seeds you can ask for information at your local flower shop(s) or go online and look for seeds there. Now that you know the two types of Damiana plants it will be easy to identify and get the correct seeds easily.

**For best sexual performance and increased potency look for:**

*"Buy Turnera Aphrodisiaca Damiana seeds"* on any major search engine online.

At the time of writing this I just made a search and found a pack of <u>10 Damiana seeds</u> (equals to 10 plants) <u>for about $10</u>.

After you have all the materials ready you must first sow the Damiana seeds in the soil. Fill the pots with the soil. Then Sow the seed a few centimeters/inches below the soil surface in each pot (experiment with the depth, it doesn't have to be too deep down the pot).

Water the pots very carefully (spraying water is recommended). Make sure the soil offers good drainage and that the seeds are below the soil surface.

The pots (especially during germination), should be placed outside the house only on hot seasons. Remember, this plant flourishes in hot climates.

You only have to wait until the Damiana seeds germinate (2-5 weeks) while you will see the plant coming out of the soil surface and grow.

Again, do not place the young plants in places with low temperatures and they need as much sun light as you can give them.

And all that's left to do is water the plant every day, let it grow and then enjoy it (usually in tea form).

## The plant blossoms late Spring until late Summer. Repeatedly!

When you have your nice seedling(s), you can follow the instructions described in previous step and transplant the plants to a larger pot or garden (see below)...

If you live in hot climates then you can transplant some Damiana plants outside in your garden. You will create an amazing view in your house/garden plus remember all the **aphrodisiac**

**benefits** from all the parts of the plant that should be collected and dried to create the tea.

You can also have the Damiana plant(s) in pot(s) inside the house during cold seasons and move them outside in your garden/backyard when the weather gets hotter. You can also transplant them into your garden's soil.

**And this is how to grow this magical plant, Damiana, from seeds. It's not difficult at all! Did I mention it blooms repeatedly?**

I consider it the best choice for a garden or any place where flowers grow. The beautiful yellow Damiana flowers will definitely make a difference wherever they are placed (as long as it's hot and sunny!)

**But I guess you are much more interested for its aphrodisiac effects right?**

So.... Now, let's see how to consume the lovely Damiana...

# Step 3: How to Consume Damiana and Boost Sexual Performance

You can consume almost every part of the plant (except the roots!) dried in tea form.

The shrub which has a strong spicy odor contains significant amounts of essential oils.

The leaves make a great relaxing and aphrodisiac tea. The Damiana leaves are also used to make incense with aphrodisiac effects (it is said to attract members of the opposite sex like crazy).

You can make a tea from a mixture of all parts of the plant (shrub, leaves, and flowers) apart from the root system. The mixture should be 100% dried.

(**Important**: Most people only use dried leaves and maybe flowers to make the aphrodisiac tea)

The ancient Mexican recipe is Damiana leaves and flowers tea plus as much raw (brown) sugar as you like added for best sexual performance!

But there are recent scientific studies too [1]. These have shown evidence of increased sexual activity in animals (both male and female species).

So it is a proven fact that if you consume Damiana often, you will increase your sexual potency in unimaginable levels!

Do not fall on the category of people who consume chemical drugs (like v.i.a.g.r.a) to boost sexual performance - There's always a better natural alternative.

**And in the case of aphrodisiacs, Damiana is the absolute Queen. Consume it responsibly.-**

# Resources

Herbs, oils and other aphrodisiacs!
Highly recommended, please visit this
link:
http://hyperdeals.biz/go/17/

## More aphrodisiac offers? See this:

http://aphrodisiac.webs.com/apps/links/

Damiana in Wikipedia:

http://en.wikipedia.org/wiki/Damiana

# Legal issues

As mentioned in the beginning of this book, growing Damiana is forbidden in certain states or countries. Make sure your country belongs to the majority of countries who will not even consider of declaring Damiana as an illegal plant.

The reason why growing Damiana became illegal in some places is because of the 100% lethal and illegal drug with the name *"Black-Mamba"* which actually holds the name of one of the most lethal snakes in the world. This drug included Damiana extracts and became extremely popular in the UK (and US also). As a result the growing of Damiana was forbidden.

I, the author of this book cannot be held responsible if you perform any illegal actions as a result of reading this book!

# THE END

# References

[1] Regarding the effects of Damiana on animals

*** **Arletti, R., Benelli, A., Cavazzuti, E., Scarpetta, G., & Bertolini, A.** (September 1998), *"Stimulating property of Turnera diffusa and Pfaffia paniculata extracts on the sexual behavior of male rats"*, Psychopharmacology 143: 15–19

*** **Estrada-Reyesb, K.R., Ortiz-Lópeza, P., Gutiérrez-Ortíza, J., & Martínez-Mota, L.** (June 2009), *"Turnera diffusa Wild (Turneraceae) recovers sexual behavior in sexually exhausted males"*, Journal of Ethnopharmacology 123: 423–429

# Credits

To my lovely editor Lazaros who made this book come true just for me. Look at his books:

http://amazon.com/author/lazarosgeorgoulas

## All images from Wikimedia Commons:

http://commons.wikimedia.org

Intro: H. Zell
Step 2a: H. Zell

**Herbs, oils and other aphrodisiacs!
Highly recommended,go here:**

http://hyperdeals.biz/go/17/

>>>> Would you like to see more of my books? Go to my author central on Amazon:

http://amazon.com/author/mariamarkella